*The Ac.*

A freelance writer ever since he won the Gregory Award in 1974, Roger Garfitt has been Poetry Critic of *London Magazine*, Editor of *Poetry Review*, Writing Fellow at the University of East Anglia, and Royal Literary Fund Fellow at Swansea University. He runs a Poetry Masterclass for the University of Cambridge Institute of Continuing Education at Madingley Hall. He was married to Frances Horovitz, whose *Collected Poems* he edited for Bloodaxe after her early death from cancer. From 1985 to 1992 he spent much of his time in Colombia and his *Selected Poems* (Carcanet, 2000) includes despatches that first appeared in *Granta* and *London Review of Books*. Now remarried and living in the Shropshire Hills, he performs Poetry & Jazz with Nikki Iles and the John Williams Octet. *In All My Holy Mountain*, their celebration of the life and work of Mary Webb, is available on CD from www.jazzcds.co.uk. His memoir, *The Horseman's Word*, (Jonathan Cape, 2011) was shortlisted for the PEN/Ackerley Prize. His previous collections from Carcanet include *Given Ground* (1989), which was a Poetry Book Society Recommendation.

ROGER GARFITT

# *The Action*

CARCANET

First published in Great Britain in 2019 by
Carcanet Press Ltd
Alliance House, 30 Cross Street
Manchester M2 7AQ
www.carcanet.co.uk

A CIP catalogue record for this book is available from the British Library.
ISBN 978 1 784107 71 0

The publisher acknowledges financial assistance from Arts Council England.

Typeset in England by XL Publishing Services, Exmouth
Printed and bound in England by SRP Ltd, Exeter

*For Margaret*

*I am listening to the tap shoes*
*you should have been given as a girl,*
*your feet finding you just in time, time*
*to shuffle, to brush back on your heel*
*and ease out into the buffalo, the swing*
*of those long, stage-crossing strides*
*you could never quite suppress, even*
*on the* tut-tut-tut *of the library floor.*

# Contents

# Ladywell

It busies up out of the summer night
the moment we turn off the TV: birling
of water that was the Mesolithic

for survival, word of mouth from
the first foragers to the flint traders
on the ridgeway: *Drop down*

*to the spring line!* Where the Romans
were glad enough to drink too,
though she seemed more maenad

than nymph, this spirit even the ice
could not still, driven as the white petals
that broke from the blackthorn.

The monks tried to gentle her, *Our
Lady's Well*, as they drew the water
for their beadhouse on the hill.

Generations came down to drink
after Mattins, or to fill the font
for a christening. But what ravels

under the siltstone arch will pass
the Atlantic through the harebell
and still not rest.

# Lesser Celandine

The leaves take up their spadework
in the dead of the year, subsisting
like cottagers on their flitch of bacon
on the sugars stored in the long fingers
of the roots, the figs they don't give
for frost.

          They farm the first sunlight,
gathering enough from the darker bands
in the spectrum, the red and the blue,
to forge their own sunrise, those blades of gold
Wordsworth imagined firing a *workman*
*worthy to be sainted, the first to*
*set the sign-board in a blaze.*

          Canny blades,
though, that fold over the flowerhead
in wind and rain, one with the labourer
huddled under his coat, the bee's first nectar
as precious as body heat, all the generations
of survival as our face of the earth finally
turns towards the sun.

# Snowdrop

Think of it waiting
           the hard weather out
keeping that lilt to
           itself, that tremor
in the close court
           of the bell

Think of the stillness
           in the sober sides
the steadfast silence
           of the meeting house
Quaker heads bowed
           in patience

Think of the lightness
           it has held in trust
that wingbeat of green
           the petticoats show
when the stiff skirts
           lift at last

## Daffodils

*variations on an image from Michael O'Higgins*

Something is fettling
in the summer heat

smoothing into the crease
of a muzzle

whittling to the tip
of an ear

a long head raised
underground

looking to leap from
year to year


Something is bridling
at the winter cold

the stamp of a hoof
in the hard earth

the changle of a bit
in the frost

some deep chest drawn
into harness

when all impetus
is lost

Something is pulling
into the late spring

neck upon neck
bent to the shaft

and the same sweat
on every one

the horse's heads
of gold

that draw the chariot
of the sun

## Bloodshot Daisies

Anemone red,
so deep it's almost magenta,
but more steely, more
heartfelt.

In daisies
it's a blooding
of their innocent blades,
a maenad colour

that lets slip
how fierce the dark months are
when Persephone mates
with Hades.

## The Touch

A finger of sun
in the fork of an ash
finds the green hearts
of the violets, so down-
cast from a late spring
they incline to the moss
they are rooted in,
all their sugars gone,
until the gradual touch
of the light, implicit,
insistent, cajoles them
and they cup open, greedy
as the Sheela-na-Gig, or
the flowers' Alexandrian
blue, the top two petals
pulled back to show
the cuckoo's shoe.

# Dogroses

When they lifted from the palings
and their pinks floated thin as air
over grey wood and twisted wire,

I was blooded, as the huntsman,
but with tenderness,
wild with it and never guessing

wilderness could hold renewal,
the dogroses fold over
until they fold into the rose.

## Harebell

Almost bare of blue,

a blown egg
of colour,

a shell sculling

on the tide-race
of air,

it catches you

unawares, an after-
image that floats up

out of nowhere,

doubling you back
in disbelief

to the sheen of ice

or honesty, the petals
fluted in Gothic plate

and the silicate

of blue there is no
imagining,

a breath taken

from the thin soils
of the edge,

a semitone

the earth, crouched
over its elbow pipes,

has wrestled clear.

# The Misgiving

The rowans have lit up along the ridgeway,
such rifts of colour they might be in Hungarian
traditional dress, their berries worn as so many favours
over so many layers, their fringed shawls floating
over embroidered depths.

Persephone descends in the fullness of her power.

So why do I glimpse loops of braid over forester's green
and pennons stream the length of the ridgeway?
Why are the colours so brave? And why do so many
ride down to their deaths?

# The Hackle

All five foot of him stretches up to the hackle
on his beret, the white plume tipped with red
that bloods him as a Fusilier
and might be his avatar.

He holds his tin outside the Metro station,
all a-shimmer in his army cadet uniform,
as if he were still downloading,
                the green bars running up

to the battle honour. Dreams of the chances
he will take, exceptional and intent
as if he were rising to a header
                in the goal mouth.

And of his place in the homecoming parade,
his face in the long curve of pride
as the battalion enjoys
                the freedom of the city.

When did he sign up? Was it in the half-light
of a front parlour, the ribbon of a DCM
glimmering between his fingers,
                dark blue and crimson?

Or in the brilliant light of a photo, such laughter
from the three young men in their khaki shirts
that he could not wait
                to be in on the joke?

# Among the Believers

*'God is still in motion'*
– Gerrard Winstanley

Gospel oak, the close grain of their voices
as they sing for the brother they will see
in the Kingdom. I could shelter in their lee,
in their obduracy, shoulder to shoulder
with the pikemen at Naseby, step by step
with Pilgrim on the Hill Difficulty,
if the animal in me did not hear
a relish, a resonance in the throat:
it brews as if they were saddling up
to smite the Amalekites, the holy
mountain only glimpsed through slaughter,
and God no longer *in motion*. Shall we
inherit the Kingdom? We might have had
the whole earth as a common treasury.

# IED

Focus is all. To see only the wires
he has to cut, the fine lines in the dust
that would have the hearses brought to a halt
for the throwing of flowers, the widows
take slow steps at the Festival of Remembrance
and the Queen give a silver pin for their lapel.

He paces. And crouches, choosing where to angle
the cutters, as if he and his fathers before him
were not hardwired into the blindness of this place,
the agency that brought down the visionary King
just another throw in the Great Game, and his own death,
if he fails to read the signs, a secondary
of Empire, like the child bride brutalised
in a cellar, or the woman whose crime was to be raped.

*Note:* King Amanullah Khan, whose far-reaching reforms would have
transformed Afghanistan and introduced education for women, was deposed in
1929 when British agents stirred up the tribes against him.

# Spain

*for Patience Edney*

They sit in a cave with a hundred beds,
the nurse from St Albans and the mayor
who ferries food from the village below.
She hears the last intake of troops singing
as they go up to the Front, 'children' of
fifteen or sixteen. 'I became a man,'
he tells her, 'when the land reform came in.
I measured the plots. I learned to read and
write.'

His words are an earnest of the new earth
that had brought men to the Gare d'Austerlitz
in their Sunday suits, brown paper parcels
under their arms, a faith she must hold to
against the atavism of the Stuka's howl,
even as the children sing to their deaths.

# The Sweat

The specialist shadows the bombmaker,
reads his devotion in his DNA,
in the drop of dried sweat on the casing
that gives another print-out of patience
and prayer. Imagines a desert faith,
absolute light, where once there might have been
the play of water in a walled garden
and one facet glancing off another.

Does not dwell on that other specialist
who engineered a coup, on the techniques
brought in to 'manage' a democracy,
the interrogation cells that reset
its DNA. *A desert faith*, he thinks,
one absolute glancing off another.

# Two Photographs

*in memory of Sheila Pearson*


### *i*   The Child

These eyes would look steadily from under their red riding hood,
reading each turn of the path as she takes it, each tree shadow
she passes through, so composed in her small self that the forest
takes her for one of its own, the wolf is unnerved and slopes off.

So much in store for her.  But she has stored so much already.
The eyes brim with depth, as if she has absorbed all the tales told
on a winter's night, all the pluck of those who had to make their
own luck, as she will when she comes to pick her way through the paths.


### *ii*   The Bride

In these eyes a path has opened that could run straight from Eden,
the leaves barred with gold as if they were finches, the light so quick
they might be goldcrests.
                    There had been the discipline of the eyes,
lowered before the ward sister. And there had been a cradling
in the eyes, dark with concern as they bent over a sick child.
This was the chosen path, the calling.
                                 But there are surprises
on the path, places where a crossroads has all its old power.
A nurse meets a nurseryman and suddenly a green lane
runs from Eden
                  the air so alive with finches that half a
century on we can still feel them fly
                                 or were they goldcrests?

# Outside

*a memory of Frances*

You take off your gloves, spread your fingers
to the air. Anonymous for a moment,
let yourself be turned into a bay tree.

Recover it all: the courtyard's lease of light,
the bracketing warmth of the brick,
and something subtler, something like

the invisible punch of a tuning fork
that keys you into oxygen pulses,
sucklings of honey, scent notes released

from the rose. Slip through the chemistry
of the leaves, become the eyes of the uprush,
a quickness in the air that seems alive

to itself. You push the gloves aside,
lean forward over the table, one foot braced
against the other, gathering pace.

# The Calm

*for Tristram and Anne Robson*

There is the tension of
the strings, bronze
braced against willow

until every note
is sovereign
and rings true,

and there is the calm
in the fingers, time
for every note

to find its feet
in the lordless dance
and be lost in the joy

of it. I remember
your calm, Tristram.
when all the joy in us

had died. You bent to
the harp as Brocard said,
'May she rest in peace',

and found a lament that
would lead us down to
the still waters – but not

to leave us there. One note
sprang on, as if spirit
alone could act as

a causeway. Another
leaped from it, as if the strings
were a strength in themselves.

Interval by interval, gleam
by nailed gleam, you brought us
out of the shadow,

binding the pulse back
into the body, tight
as the matador's wraps

under his suit of lights,
setting our feet on the ground
as if they struck fire

in passing. And then the notes
lifted, not for joy
but for the possibility

of joy, and the dance stepped
through us, so defiant
that I wish you calm even

now, as the chemo silts up
the spirit, the calm
and the cunning to set

in place every string
of a double harp won back
from exile and silence.

# *The Action*

*in memory of Alan Hawke*

　　　　　　　　　　　Slow work,
you would think, building... I never knew
it could be so passionate until you threw
your fast bowler's back into plastering
our living room wall.

　　　　　　　　　　Some spell
you put in that afternoon, one continual
shoulder roll of the hawk over the
wall until it was sheer in the
original sense and shone.

　　　　　　　　　　That night
from the sofa you'd glimpse it again,
run up on a spliff and a couple
of cans and throw yourself
into oblivion.

　　　　　　　　　　The long
back gathering to its pitch – that's how
your sister was these last six months,
insistent she should drive so she
didn't have to think,

　　　　　　　　　　the runs
to the hospice easier to focus on, for all
the roadworks, the overnight closures,
the diversions through small towns
in the small hours, than the

one thought
running under everything – or they were
until stalled headlights on Clee Hill
showed a lad thrown
off his motorbike.

Strange how
the perception altered in those months
that were like living on the run,
services to services, fuelled
up on double shots,

time as
tangible as the road surfaces worn
under our wheels. I see myself
now as one of those lads you
coached, learning to hold

speed in,
to pace my run over the changing
ground as if nothing could
throw the arm off
its deliberate arc.

# Herb Bennet

*for Margaret in a dark time*

It is one of the moments
when the meek inherit the earth,
the unalloyed gold of their stars

in the hedgebank. 'Yellow strawberries'
they called them in Somerset
and you can see why: but their sweetness

lay in the root, in the air of cloves
in the clothes press that drove
the devil away. So I summon them now,

the blessed herbs of our boggy patch,
the herbs bennet. Their good spirits
gather by the stream, they crowd over

the flagstone bridge, for they know
when one of their own is discountenanced,
and they would pay a queen's ransom for you.

## Dandelion

Not the lion-toothed leaves
but the flower's lion heart,
its unruly sun

        that rises
where it shouldn't, universal scamp,
urchin energy.

        Twelve years
and still it surprises us.

        Twelve years
and still the lawns have their gypsies,
their wild springs.

## Cyclamen

Smoke-trails of violet-pink

like intimacies tested
in a wind tunnel

or colours seen
with the fingertips

these are the flowers
of free fall

of that first decision
to live headlong

the Winged Victory I glimpsed
as you wrestled your sweater off

## Goldilocks

Innocent even of itself, it flowers
as four petals or five, or throws up
a bare stalk, a solar flare
from a cauldron of unknowing,

so prone to change it can only be rooted
in a quantum universe, so provisional
it could almost be human; which is why
I have chosen it for you now as the clown

becomes a granny – or Granny gets
another chance to play the clown? The petals
open, uncertain as always, and their colour,
look, is the same unguarded gold.

*Note:* Goldilocks is a species of Buttercup that is still evolving and the only species that is not poisonous.

## Winter–Flowering Jasmine

Given a high wall
and enough winters to scale it,

a century, perhaps,
of runnels and frost cracks,

it will skitter down
in its own spray,

dancing stars to left
and right, soft,

powdery-yellow stars,
first flower of the world,

innocent as the day
is young.

## Vahine

'Carter's Tested Seeds' we used to call that
polyester dressing gown I would slip
off your shoulder as if it were
wild silk,

everyday yellows and reds you drew
on as cat's eye, as cinnabar
for the hour *entre chien
et loup*,

the colours lying on you so lightly
you were hardly dressed at all,
or only in the heat of
your skin.

## The Other Company

Once in a month of Sundays
it draws up,

not the familiar bus
built of misgivings,

whose engine labours
under a rattle of flaps,

whose exhaust is a spew
of midnight oil,

but the well-tempered bus
riveted with light,

the bus that pulls in
out of nowhere,

with just one seat left
on the long bench.

Particular honour is paid on Parnassus
To those whose time is not just their own. Take your place
Among the wits by which imagination lives.

# A Dryad of the Sacred Wood

*for Emma Young*

A slip of sunlight between trees

a hint of sawdust on a cobweb
from a squirrel's footfall overhead

a woodpecker's elegant abseil
down the bark of a Douglas fir

*Wate, wate, cur-cur* is the alarm
of the nightingale

but this path has only
the wren's flit

the pied wagtail's flicker
a harry of goldfinches

as you come into the clear

## Homecoming

Blue softens the air.
The curlew's echo lifts,
longing, belonging…

# After the Great Storm

Wind shear tore sleep away with the tiles.
Looked out at the parking lot
– it had turned back into Paradise.

But the car was still there, long shadow
under the handstand of a pine branch.
Get to London or lose a day's work!

Strange how regular the shockwaves were,
the trees along the coast road reduced
to a pattern in flock wallpaper.

Still in the twentieth century,
an overrider in his sealed pod,
I turned onto the A23

and found myself back in the greenwood,
shadow where the carriageway had been
and the ridged bark of a fallen tree.

Then a shine to my right – two tyre tracks
of flattened grass – someone had slipped
over the central reservation,

as if instinct had been there all along,
only awaiting its chance to awake.
I drove against an absence of traffic,

the morning light still quick on creatures
out of their element, their windward twigs
chamfered to a millimetric gleam,

so alive had they been to the air.
One by one, I passed them, a gnat's whine
through their stillness, and came on a trunk

there was no passing, its snapped-off roots
high overhead, and a policeman
scaled down to a manikin waving me

round the back of it, the carriageway down
to a forest path and the tyres pressing
as though theirs were the first footfall.

# An Innocent

The frog by the coal bunker
is breathing night
breathing the damp of it

such translucency
such trust in its pear skin
that something permeates

even my unperceiving
a suppleness in the air
off the Atlantic

frogs have sheltered in
since the meltwaters dispersed
the Gulf Stream steadied

and the frost lifted    the frost
of strange pollen    of pale
tundra flowers

Water salts and sinks    draws up
warmth in a stream stronger
than any river    than all the

Atlantic's rivers braided
together    and the frog
breathes on    the skin so clear

as it rebalances    such a pulse
of electrolytes across
the membrane    that the

scuttle in my hand
grows heavy    heavy
with the cloud cover where

a fungus might form

# Four Butterflies

*for Nadia Kingsley*

### i *Dark Green Fritillary*

A harlequin's flicker from knapweed
to thistlehead, orange glanced with black
warning enough to stay out of the chase,
the slapstick that will see it mate
in a moment and score twice, a coupled pair
with both heads still drilling for nectar:

but catch it unawares, wings closed
to disclose the green, the furry
underwood green, and it's an old god
you glimpse, who will crawl on his belly
unafraid, who will feed on the dog-violet
through moult after moult to dissolve
into the dark of the pupa, the pulse
where it forms upside-down, folded
energy that can only press into song
or shake out into flight.

## ii  *Marbled White*

Eats its own shell on hatching
secret agent bundling away her parachute

and goes to ground in the grass
wintering on nothing but itself

Grows cautious as the light grows
and feeds only at night

a stem thickening in the Tor Grass
and the Yorkshire Fog

Only to roll as its own dice
on the bare earth    the one

of itself thrown to chance
and come up as wings spread

to the sun    a double six
in a run of luck    and take off

into its variations    move through its
mirrorings to the end

of light

### iii  *Wall*

It has come to rest in the language
as it might on a breadth of drystone,
just enough for it to sunbathe on
its own shadow, wings two-thirds open
as the blood heat builds. Will it lift back
into the margin, the hinterland
we take for granted, scrap of colour
that says *sumer is icumen-in?*
(Though it goes back beyond us, goes back
to *vallum*, the Latin for 'rampart',
a word the Saxons or the Anglo-
Frisians *(the Anglo-Frisians!)*
must have found useful as they squatted
among the ruins.) Or will it lift,
*wallflower of the fort, little brooch*
*of the stone*, into a place that has
no margins, no time for frippery?

iv   *Red Admiral*

We never dreamed they were gypsy colours,
those bands of red where earth brown
shades into black and black
flashes white and has a sheen of blue.
We never saw *tzigane* in that orange hem.

Someone would shout 'Red Admiral!'
and it was as if an ensign were flying
beyond the ring of marbles or the first
conker fights, a cutaway from history
you could catch and cup in your palm,

the trembling of its wings a kiss
like Hardy's, an initiation
into the band of brothers. You hesitated
to let it go, to become a star on the chest
or a bloodstain on the quarterdeck.

We never suspected it had flown out of
its own deep song, the innate impulse
that sent its forefathers north in the spring,
Roma who would mate over the ivy clumps
of a new island. Or that those colours

unfurled from a tent in the nettles, those zags
of red flickering over the apples we scrumped
from back gardens, would have to be struck
against the trunk of a tree, the bark of
its underwings turn ghostly in the frost.

## Prisoner of War Work

*from Norman Cross Prison, Peterborough*

All around him men are gambling
their rations away.

He keeps his head down, waits
for first light between the bars

to return him to the afternoon
he is working towards, his scale model

of a day like any other. So far off now
he had to set it like a loft of heaven

over two great wheels, each of them
a storey high, as if that's all home was,

a platform over the world's engines
– or his skill and patience over

the good people of Peterborough,
whose generosity he must harness

as the miller harnesses the stream.
Others are building spinning jennies,

as if in deference to the industry
that has given England the edge,

one even a miniature guillotine,
which seems an admission too far.

If he's to bring guineas home to
La Belle France, let them be

in tribute, the teeth he cuts
into the bone of the wheels

so precise they interlock,
the wheels so finely balanced

they revolve in equipoise
on an afternoon so still

he can hear the trickle
of a wheel

as his mother spins,
the movement of a clock

as his wife rocks
the cradle, all driven by

a handle a child could turn.

The truce is over. The firing begins again.
How strange it was, crouched beneath the parapet,
to hear the tune I used to sing at Father's elbow
in the family pew. How intimate it always seemed,
that last verse, *to be sung on Christmas Day*,
'Yea, Lord, we greet thee, Born this happy morning',
as if our voices might carry all the way back
to Bethlehem. We sang it so quietly yesterday,
as if they were family too. And I thought back
to Harvest Festival as a boy, glancing down
to find **Wir pflügen und wir streuen** set over
'We plough the fields, and scatter...' Did they paint
their waggons different colours? With us every county
had its own. What shape did they give their harvest loaves?
I imagined all the parishes of Northern Europe
in procession, horkey boughs carried from every twist
and turn of the map, and over us a phrase of Luther's
that had already caught my eye: **Ein' Feste Burg**,
'A safe stronghold our God is still...' What should I sing
across this wasted land as the shells burst and the snipers
pick us off? 'A deep dug-out our God is now'?

# The Hedger's Mittens

*in memory of George Stokes*

When his leather mittens became too stiff to use,
the old man explained, he'd bury them in the ground
for a spell, *put them back to Old England...*

the voice gentling as he trusted *the nature of*
*the soil'd bring the nature back into the mitten.*
I was left to wonder at the depth of that trust

where I felt only an absence, the absence of
all those young men Kitchener had pointed
the finger at, who were sent white feathers

if they didn't join up. What company can I find
for their cancelled lives? Just the witness of Owen
and Sassoon. Just the duress of Ivor Gurney.

Voices raised out of the cross-grain of England,
out of the questioning that won our common ground,
not to disavow that old man and his gentle trust

but to enlist them, as England turns ungentle once more.

# The Oldest Script

*Six poems from a Year of the Artist Residency
at Acton Scott Historic Working Farm*

### i   The First Mark
*for James Plant*

*'In blacksmithing
it's not the last mark
of the hammer
that shows,
it's the first
two or three blows.*

*Get those right, and
the rest of it flows.*

*Get them wrong, and half
the day goes,
fudging and finicking about...'*

– as if there is a knack
sudden as luck, a moment
when time can be turned

and the spear proves true
to its foreshadowing
on the wall of the cave

or the knapping of flakes
from a flint core gives us
the run of the earth.

## ii *High Cut*
### *for Jim Elliott*

Drawn like blades of earth, the ridges catch light
out of a dull sky. Half-crouched, his arms wide
to the plough handles, a man stalks them as they shear
from the mouldboard. Every other pace
he halts the horses, takes a long spanner
from his back pocket and tightens the outrigging
of press wheel and boats, keels of metal that he draws
on chains, furrow-sharpeners that ride in his wake.

He is the first scribe, perfecting the oldest script.
All alphabets go back to tallies, harvest yields
scratched on clay. The first lines were the lines of increase.
And the shieldwall of books? Breathing spaces we won
when warrior farmers marked out their battleline,
their ridges exact, drawn like blades of earth.

iii   *The Traveller*
*for Andrew Lane*

Poor traveller,
that never travels...

Monk
of the circumference
making its only circuit,
it is trundled around the rim
of each new wheel, each return
of the chalk mark on its little wheel
counted off under the breath: one foot,
two foot, three...

Vanishing term,
it sets up the equation
that has iron stretched in a ring of fire
and shrunk around a wheel over a water pit,
quarter of an inch smaller in circumference
for every foot of diameter.

Patient tuner,
it works towards a note
three woods can make on the stones of a yard:
elm of the hub, ash of the felloes, cleft oak of the spokes,
all driven together in a hoop of iron, all caught up
in the spring of a wheel.

iv  *The Bootlace*
*for Vernon Warwick*

Each summer, to mark his arrival,
his grandfather would stoop, draw the lace
from his boot and tie it to the bridle,

his braid of office. Six hands taller,
he would lead the Shire from the stable,
the staddle-stones of its hooves falling

into step, becoming the blood-beat
of a drum, a bass note through the earth
that seemed to muster under their feet,

dark green the brocade of the clover
in the homespun of the hay. They were
drawing the sun's cart, harvest heaped over

its yellow boards. The old man was a legend:
he could lift loads that broke the pikel,
haystorms the boy could scarcely tread-in

before the next blacked-out the roundel
of the loft. But what brings him to mind
is the bindertwine he had wound through

his boot: half-thrift, half-ceremony,
it gave a boy his most prized belonging,
his place in the harvest company.

v   *The Searcher*
*for Tom Williamson*

His bent back listens
to the weight
he has shouldered,

his hand to the foot
he has folded
into his lap. Hardness

under the thumb. Dead spot
in the give
of the hoof. And hidden

so the farrier must be
the conjuror
once more. In so deep

only the thin blade
of the searcher
can slip, a steeled nerve,

between the wall and the blood.

## vi  *The Goose Quill*
*in memory of Ossie Morris*

The hazel rod nosedives,
dead wood in your hands,

the pulse of water lost
to a blank face of rock.

It is the summer of '76
and the beasts are moaning

from thirst. You swing the stick
up along the side of the quarry,

pick away two or three stones
and there is a wrinkle of water,

*no thicker than a grub.*

The farmer screws a goose quill
into the rock, leaves a bucket

to chirr all summer with that
thin piping.

We need these stories
as a generation goes

that had learned to hold on
by a thread. Old improviser,

remind us of the hidden pulses.
Tell us how to woo the earth

when it turns away.

# Four Poems from 'Presences of Jazz'

### i   *Young Lester*

He rolls the only dice
        at which he never loses
so quick and light the sixes
        fall beyond belief

The New Orleans Strutter
        the kid who had to Charleston
to his own horn has the room
        at his fingertips
all eyes on the freaks of touch
        that are conjuring notes
from the by-ways of the metal
        bluegrass leaps
back country blues
        and C-melodies
transposed for the tenor
        as if the paces
of the unicorn
        were to be found
in the horse

        All the accessories
are still to come
        the hieroglyphics
on his cuff-links
        the matching suede shoes
with every suit

        but already he has
his call – that little hoot
        as he goes up in the air –
and his calling
        the light tones the hipsters

will take into their cabbala
       and sing under their breath
as alive as the dust
       under the shaded lamps
of the pool room
       to the ascension
of the everyday

## ii  *Miles in Paris*

The spring before the fall,
the big coat held in close
though it's said to be May,

the cigarette shielded
in his hand, he walks on
as if a sound were

tracking him, a bass
turning on itself under
the pavement. Could not say

why he has to leave that
Egyptian face. Or those
café tables where he sits

as an equal. To glimpse her
as a note bends him
to the cellars of 52nd St,

glance back at that calm
from the outcry of Birdland,
will be to know a silence

beyond the changes, a solitude
he will shape into phrases
anyone can walk down,

the bass giving us
every consideration,
the horn held-in close,

still thinking it through.

The shadow of Sugar Ray
saw him through the nights
of cold turkey – still there

in the jabs on the mute,
the resonances that score
as he dances back. And

in the dancer on his arm,
the cool of his Italian suits
and his Ferrari. Which

will not save him from 'a
Georgia head-whipping' on
Broadway, beaten by a cop's

blackjack for taking the air
outside Birdland. A heavier
presence begins to brood

in the open horn, to draw
on the darker notes as if
Bird were camping it up

in his best British, *All right
Lily Pons. To produce beauty,
we must suffer pain – from the oyster*

*comes the pearl.* Of great price,
as the cocaine takes hold,
the dancer flees, and he's left

with the shadow of Jack Johnson.

### iv  *Mingus: Self-Portrait in Three Colours*

Not that he glances out of it, he is glancing away,
even the colours are glanced away, doubt overlays them
so that they are fired and burn back through the glaze,

anemones on a café table, arranged in a liturgy of love,
all the colours of blood against the small check of the cloth,
the blue has a premonition, there is an inkling in the red,

but the magentas pulse as they darken, still in flood,
searches rather than colours, chances of the light
as it runs the length of its wave, split seconds that give

the only glimpse of him.

# The Space

*in memory of Richard Beaumond*

Not quite the meadhall, the ballroom at Walcot Hall
where we used to meet, car-sharing poets
with cling-filmed plates for the communal lunch,
but we were glad of the space, the window seats
where we could sit *in parenthesis*, the *solvitur
ambulando* around the lake that took us past those
other solitaries, the fishermen hunched over their rods,
even the bus shelter at the end of the drive
where Michael would wait for a poem to pull in
and take him on board.

Born in the village and dancing with the Bedlams
in blackface, as once you would have been wise to
under the eyes of the gentry, it must have seemed
a glimpse of commonwealth to bring us here,
Richard, the opening of a space words could cross
and re-cross, finding forms as light and as durable
as the ark woven of rushes for the Midsummer
Rejoicing. Here's to the energy we sent through
the room, mind swinging off mind
as in Strip-the-Willow.

# Acknowledgements

My thanks are due to the editors of the following magazines in which a number of these poems were first published: *Agenda*, *Birdsuit*, *PN Review*, *Scintilla* and *Stand*.

'Snowdrop' first appeared in *The Way You Say the World*, a celebration for Anne Stevenson, edited by John Lucas and Matt Simpson and published by Shoestring Press.

'The Touch' first appeared in *Soul Feathers*, an anthology published in aid of Macmillan Cancer Support by Indigo Dreams.

'Harebell' was commissioned by Carol Ann Duffy for her anthology, *Answering Back*, published by Picador.

'Two Photographs' was commissioned by Jemma Montagu and Lucy Montgomery in memory of their mother, Sheila Pearson, and read at her funeral.

'Outside' was commissioned by David Hart as one of the Waiting Room Poems to hang in doctor's surgeries and hospital waiting rooms.

'The Calm' was written for Tristram Robson, who played at Frances's funeral. Tristram built the only copy of the Lawes Harp, an Irish double harp from the time of William Lawes, that can actually be played. It is now in the National Harp Museum in Kilkenny. When Tristram was diagnosed with a brain tumour, he married his partner, Anne, and set himself to build a second copy of the Lawes Harp because, as Anne said, the first copy was only ninety-seven percent perfect.

'The Action' was written in memory of my brother-in-law, Alan Hawke, who played in the Durham Coastal League. When he moved to Northamptonshire, he coached the lads in his local village and took them to the County Championship.

'Cyclamen' first appeared in an anthology from the Ledbury Poetry Festival.

'Goldilocks' first appeared in *Unguarded Gold*, an anthology published by Ver Poets in memory of May Badman.

'A Dryad of the Sacred Wood' first appeared in an anthology from the Wenlock Poetry Festival.

'Homecoming' was written for a poet/artist project with Noel Connor in Manchester Central Library.

'Four Butterflies' was written for *Shropshire Butterflies*, a poetry and art book edited by Nadia Kingsley and published by Fair Acre Press.

The poems in 'The Oldest Script' were written during a Year of the Artist Residency at Acton Scott Historic Working Farm. The first five are dedicated to the craftsmen who instructed me in the niceties of their craft and the sixth is in memory of an old friend and neighbour. They were first published in *Spiked*.

'Mingus – Self-Portrait in Three Colours' was first broadcast with the John Williams Septet on BBC Midlands Radio. 'Miles in Paris' and 'Miles in New York' were first performed with John Williams & Friends as part of Music at Leasowes Bank.

'The Space' – Richard Beaumond founded the Border Poets and their next anthology will be dedicated to him.